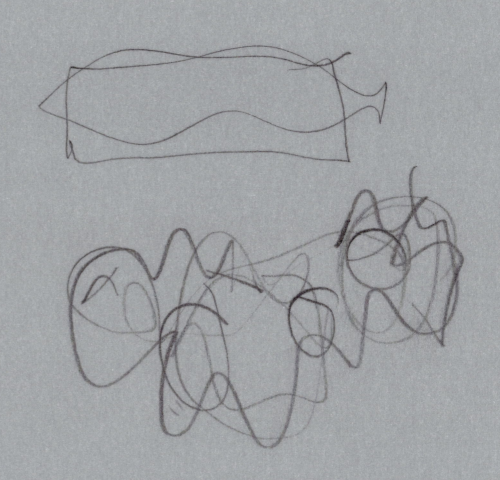

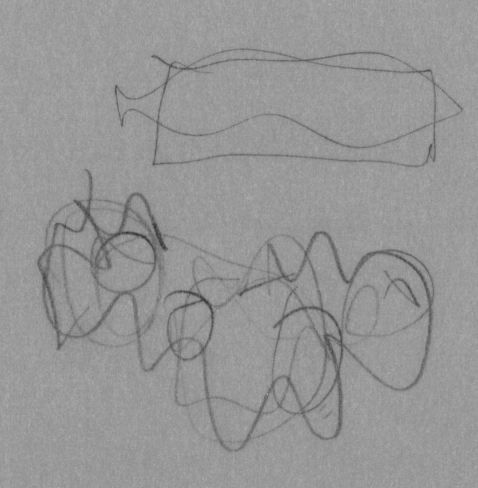

Frank Gehry Designs

The Lou Ruvo Brain Institute, Las Vegas

Las Vegas Art Museum   December 13, 2006 – March 25, 2007
Exhibition presented by Lawyer Trane

 BRIGHTCITYBOOKS

This catalog is published in conjunction with the exhibition, "Frank Gehry Designs the Lou Ruvo Brain Institute, Las Vegas," organized by Libby Lumpkin with Renee Coppola and Courtney Howerton. It appears at the Las Vegas Art Museum, December 13, 2006–March 25, 2007.

Catalog design by Skeet Link.
Catalog produced and edited under the direction of Gary Kornblau.

Las Vegas Art Museum
9600 West Sahara Avenue
Las Vegas, Nevada 89117

ISBN 0-9774861-2-5

Printed in the United States.

Cover
Study Model for the Lou Ruvo Brain Institute, 2005-06. Acrylic resin, wood, paper and glue, 6 x 11 ½ x 4 ¾ inches.

Back Cover
Final Design Development Model for the Lou Ruvo Brain Institute, November 2006. Scale 1/8" = 1'0", mixed media, 36 x 36 x 10 inches.

Front Flyleaf
Sketch for the Lou Ruvo Brain Institute, 2005-2006. Pen on paper, 11 x 17 inches.

Photography by Michael Magat.
Courtesy of Gehry Partners, LLC.

Contents

Illustrations

Unless otherwise indicated, all illustrations depict sketches, models, renderings, or plans that represent various stages in the design development of the Lou Ruvo Brain Institute. Produced in 2005 and 2006, they appear in approximate chronological order and are courtesy of Gehry Partners, LLP. A comprehensive list of illustrations is found on page 62.

Frank Gehry's Baroque Grid

Christopher Knight

The meeting table in Frank O. Gehry's office at his studio in West Los Angeles holds a study model for the Lou Ruvo Brain Institute. You'd be forgiven for not noticing it, or even for mistaking it for something else—a toy, perhaps, or some crumpled-up wad that had not yet found its way into the wastebasket. The model is made from small wooden blocks in a variety of cubic and other multifaceted geometric forms. They've been gathered up into a ball and wrapped in heavy white construction paper, die-cut into a grid pattern and glued together. The model is not large; merely the size of a couple of fists, it's generally spherical in shape. No front or back, top or bottom can be identified. The scrunched orb appears casually disheveled.

On one hand, the model is nutty—a whimsical, nonfunctional, impractical, surprising, impulsive, capricious, and distinctly odd bit of sculptural sport. No building would ever be built that looks like this. In the best sense, however, that disjunction between common expectation and perceptual surprise is emblematic of Gehry's creative process. He's known to be an architect who thinks like an artist, and painters and sculptors have provided both friendship and inspiration for 50 years. Crossing conventional properties of painting with those of sculpture has been a centerpiece of advanced art since the 1950s, and this ball of blocks bundled in paper is a hybrid that melds together two- and three-dimensional forms. Think of it as a little lump of "creative play." Its deceptive status as important source material for a prominent new building in downtown Las Vegas that is now nearing its final design stage soon becomes clear.

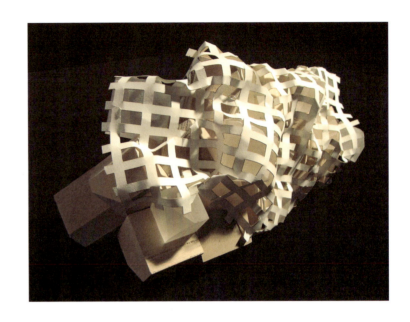

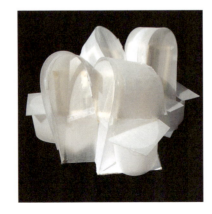

On the other hand, the seemingly eccentric Ruvo Institute model is also typical of Gehry's purely practical side. Artists don't usually have to worry about rigorously controlled and structured things like building codes, the way that architects always do, so pragmatic considerations are indispensable to the long and involved design process. One practical feature of the study model is simplicity itself: Since the spatial massing of forms is critical to every building the architect designs, the wooden blocks represent the total cubic space allotted to a particular building project. The architect's cavernous studio is filled with dozens of building and development projects he's currently working on around the world, from downtown Los Angeles to Abu Dhabi in the United Arab Emirates, all in various stages of completion. Every one of them began with similar massing studies, which recall a child's game of playing with building blocks. Gehry uses blocks so that he can arrange and rearrange spatial configurations without losing track of the overall square footage. (When it's done, the entire Ruvo building will encompass about 65,000 square feet.)

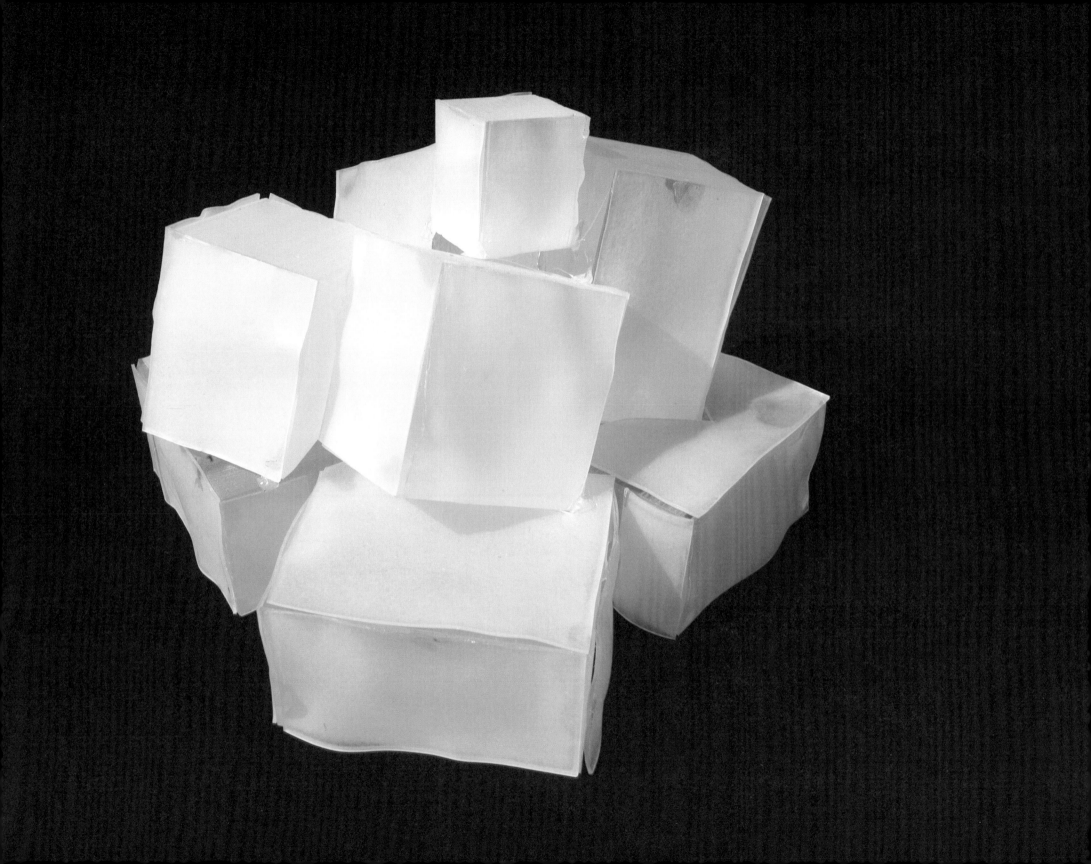

The working method is eccentric, yet sensible. The process creates pressure between rational and irrational forces—a tension that is fundamental to the design for the Ruvo Institute and to the lively power of Gehry's best work.

As a precedent, take the famous Guggenheim Bilbao, the wondrous art museum building in northern Spain whose 1997 début announced the arrival of the architectural masterpiece that would set the pace for the new millennium, making Gehry the world's most famous living architect. Looking back, an urban planner with a compass and a ruler could plot the geographic siting of the enormous building on a topographical map. A carefully drawn diagram would chart how seamlessly it fits the gentle bend in the river, while offering counterpoint to a highway bridge that curves in the opposite direction and cuts through one end of the museum. Gehry's piled-up building acts as a dynamic locus of transition: Bilbao's urban street grid is typical of 19th-century Beaux Arts design, but visually the building is linked with the hilly, organic landscape that rises up in the distance across the river.

Frank O. Gehry Guggenheim Bilbao, 1997

Similarly, an historian could list the architectural sources. They begin with the coiled rotunda of Frank Lloyd Wright's Solomon R. Guggenheim Museum in New York—the "mother ship" to Bilbao's "satellite." That building also sets a curve against a right angle. There a visitor passes from the orderly street grid of Manhattan through a small revolving door, enters a modest, low-ceilinged, compressed lobby space, and then—*whoosh!*—the big rotunda explodes into an expanding spiral, wider at the top than the bottom, which leads the eye up into a voluminous space that ends at a luminous skylight. Clean and translucent, the skylight and its geometric tracery look like a secular version of a cathedral's stained-glass rose window—a marvelously evocative representation of the modern triumph of scientific reason over religious superstition.

In Bilbao, the narrative laid out in the entry procession is different in its details, but similar in its general sequence and joyful, energetic, uplifting effect. Gehry leads a visitor downhill from the urban street grid toward the water's edge, traversing broad stairs that curve inward like the tiers of an

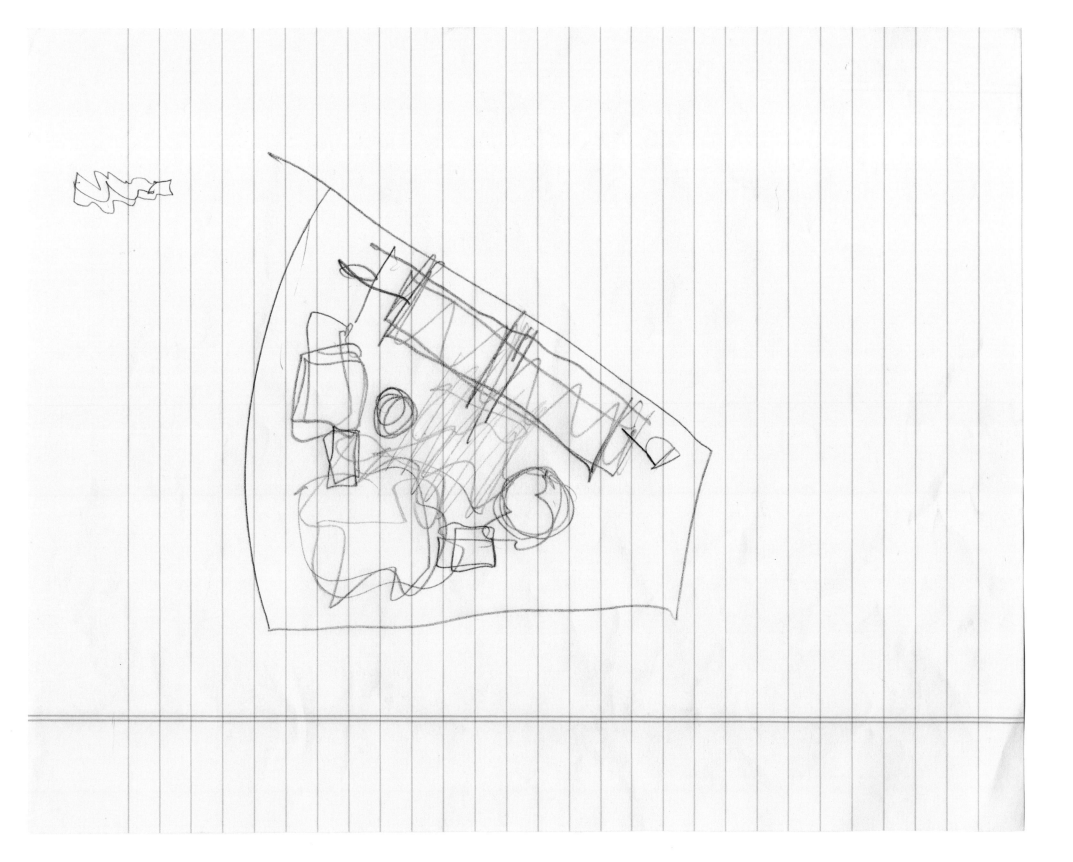

amphitheater, into a passage that steadily narrows. The building's side walls loom like limestone cliffs. The compression intensifies as one reaches the entry doors, passes inside, snakes through a tall, light-dappled walkway, and then—*whoosh!*—arrives at an enormous interior room that explodes upward into a central core. Structural elements seem to bend and splinter, like a game of pick-up sticks, as they rise to the huge building's tallest point. Bilbao borrows and transforms the New York Guggenheim's explosive entry, adapting it to a new site and circumstance.

By contrast, the specific architectural forms of Bilbao's museum would require a fabulist—or perhaps a psychiatrist—to parse. Gorgeous and gleaming, the riverside building has been likened to a burnished ship or barge, an historic source of Bilbao's obsolete sea-faring economy. (The biggest room, whose side walls curve together toward the far end like a prow, is colloquially called the "boat gallery.") In addition to that Pop iconography, the titanium skin covering much of the building's exterior also suggests the silvery scales of a fish. Gehry has used the fish-form since 1981,

for the unbuilt renovation of a house he designed in 1958-59, as well as for lamps, a restaurant in Japan, a lattice canopy anchoring a retail complex at Barcelona's Olympic Village, and more. The architect has spoken of two sources for the image. One is social, the other personal.

In the effort to scratch the Postmodern itch that arose in the 1980s, when Modernist architecture's failures had become too glaring to ignore, Gehry looked back to the primordial ooze. With tongue implanted in cheek, he considered forms that existed before humans walked the earth. He was taking cues from art. Going primordial was a starting-over tactic that American painters had used to rethink art after the devastation of Europe in World War II. Doing it tongue-in-check is a Pop art gesture; the enormous 1992 lattice fish in Barcelona, which marked a turning point for Gehry's work, recalls nothing so much as Claes Oldenburg's proposals for giant public sculptures of teddy bears and fire plugs.

Claes Oldenburg *Proposed Colossal Monument for Central Park North, New York City, Teddy Bear*, 1965

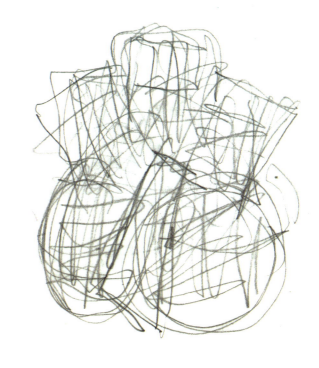

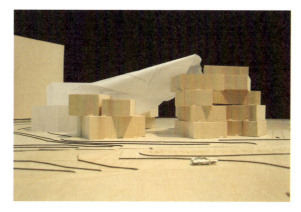
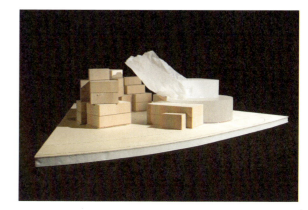

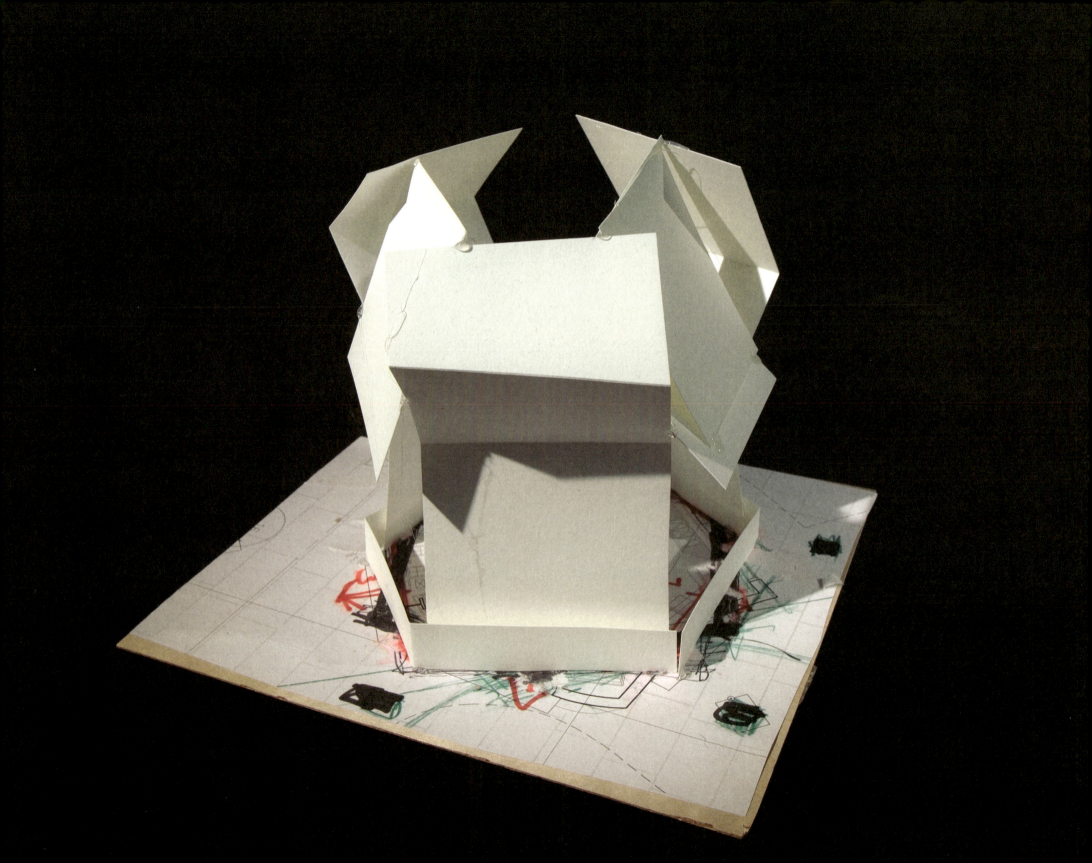

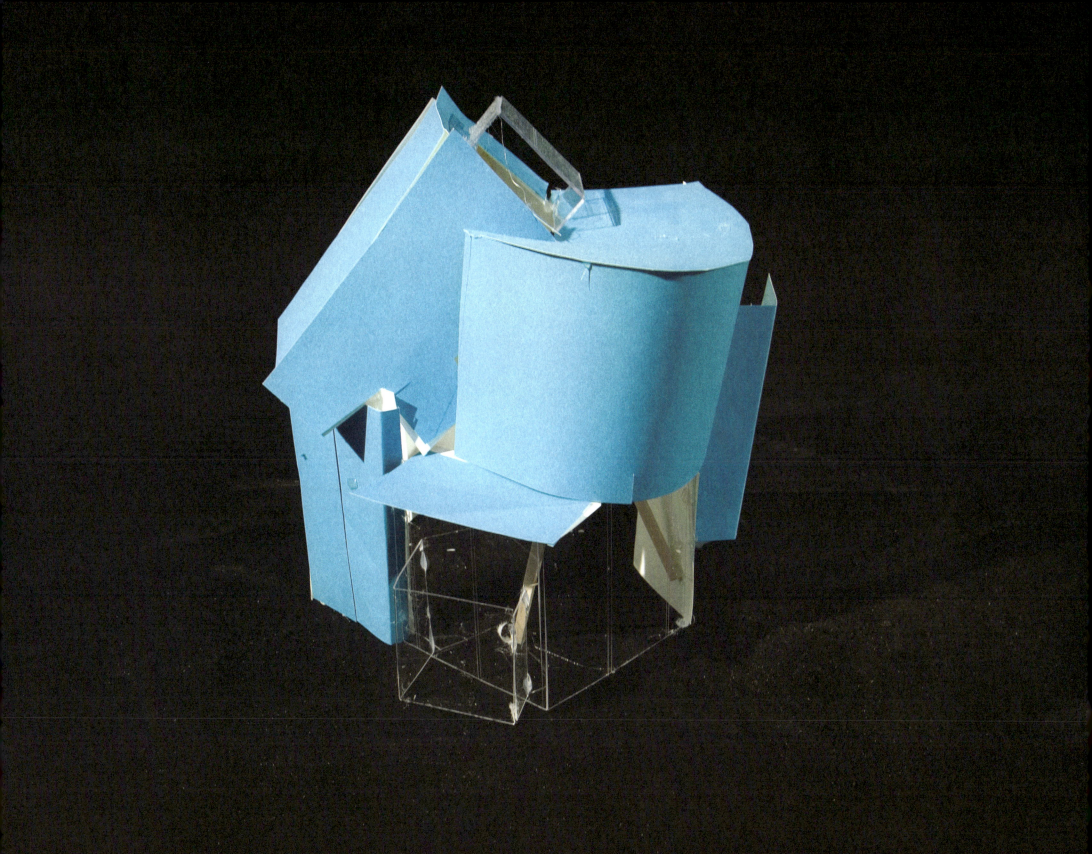

Gehry went fishing, so to speak, in Mark Rothko's *Slow Swirl at the Edge of the Sea,* the landmark 1944 painting that helped spawn Abstract Expressionism by conjuring a magical life force taking shape on a mythic shoreline. Gehry returned to the phantas- mal ordeals of childhood—to growing up poor in Toronto and seeing the live carp that his grandmother kept in the bathtub on their way to the dinner table. (For the Barcelona fish, he sensibly lopped off the tail and head.) The youthful memory haunts him, and memory is a design-element as important as any other in Gehry's work.

For the Lou Ruvo Brain Institute, named to honor the principal benefactor's father, who succumbed to Alzheimer's disease, there is pathos to the central role that fam- ily recollection so often plays in Gehry's architecture. The wife and three brothers- in-law of Dr. Milton Wexler, Gehry's long- time analyst and friend, were stricken with Huntington's disease, a related, equally

Mark Rothko *Slow Swirl at the Edge of the Sea,* 1944

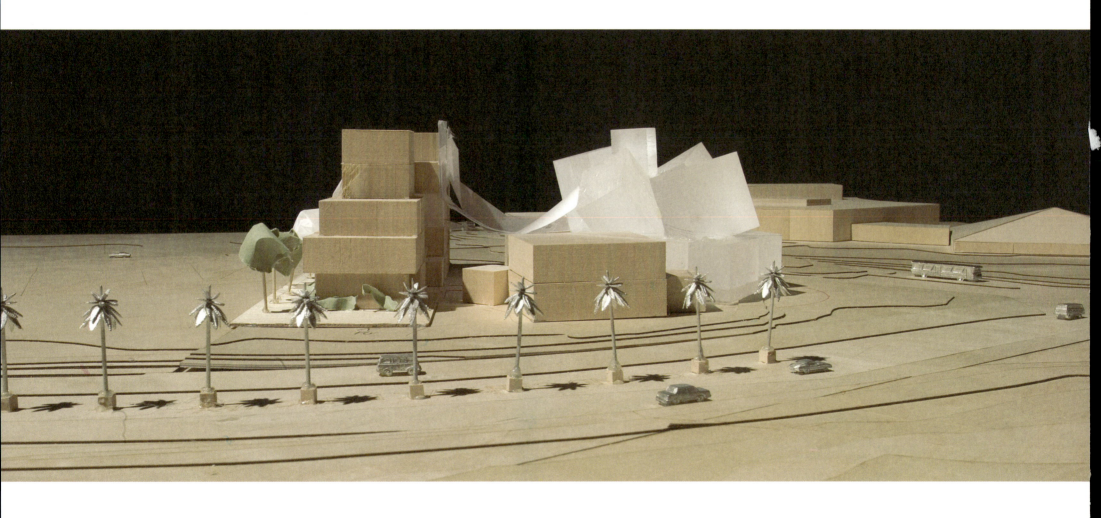

devastating neurological affliction. (The architect serves on the board of Wexler's Hereditary Disease Foundation, established to study the autosomal-dominant illness.) The Ruvo Institute will serve as the headquarters of the Keep Memory Alive Foundation and as a central clearinghouse for patients and families struggling with Alzheimer's, Huntington's, Parkinson's, and ALS diseases. The program given to the architect includes examination rooms, offices for healthcare practitioners and researchers, a "Museum of the Mind," and a community hall.

■■■

A dualism is at work in Gehry's architecture, a right-brain/left-brain tension between order, regularity, and refinement on one hand and intoxication, turmoil, and euphoria on the other. Friedrich Nietzsche, in *The Birth of Tragedy* (1872), traces the origins of this distinction to antiquity. An Apollonian view of humanity represents the rationally conceived ideal, whereas the Dionysian represents artistic conception proper, originating from humankind's subconscious. Nietzsche believes both elements are present in any work of art, with one or the other usually dominant. In periods of acute stress and social tension, like our own, the two tend to erupt in conflict.

Gehry's design for the Ruvo Institute gives unmistakable evidence of this conflict, and that dualism. It is most obvious in the community hall, housed beneath an undulating grid in stainless steel that reaches 75 feet high at its tallest point. This exciting, irregular, and exuberant space will be used for conferences and receptions. A grid is a horizontal line intersected by a vertical one, then repeated as an endless network of coordinates for locating points on an image. For a century, it has been a primary sign of Modernist abstraction. The grid forms the foundation of everything from the Suprematist and Constructivist art of the 1910s to the Minimalist and Perceptualist art of the 1960s, from which Gehry's own aesthetic first emerged. As a design motif, it is organized, orderly, machined, rational, systematic, stripped of emotionalism, and

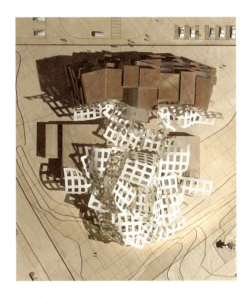

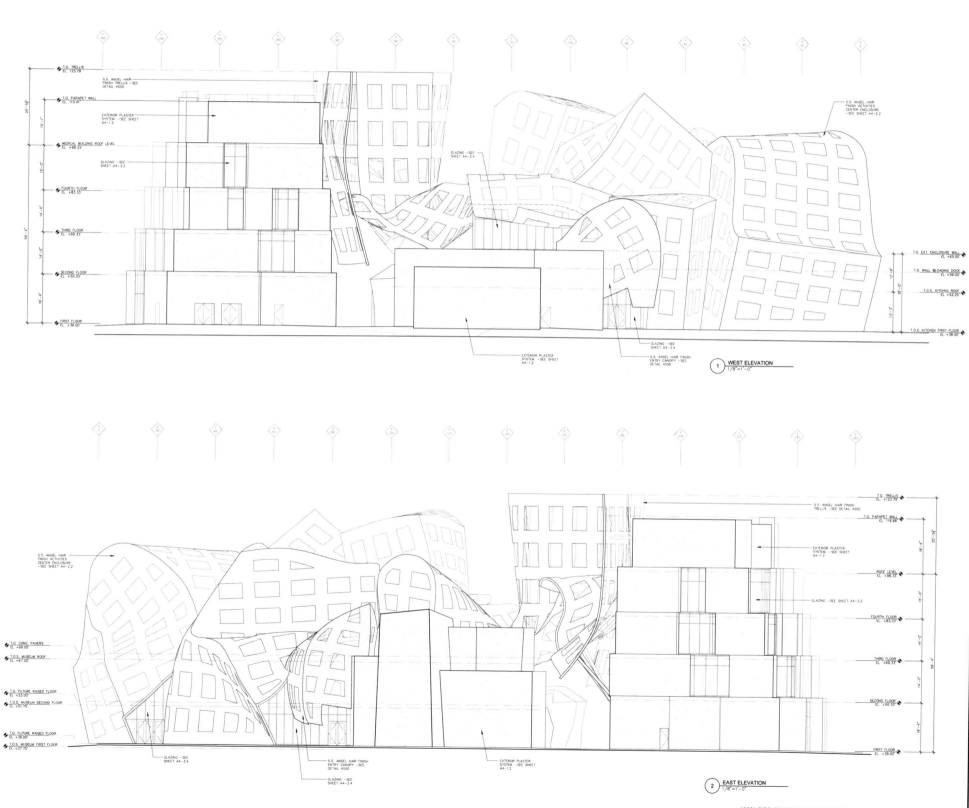

GEHRY PARTNERS, LLP.

ARCHITECT
12541 BEATRICE STREET
LOS ANGELES, CALIFORNIA 90066 USA
TEL: 310-482-3000
FAX: 310-482-3006

CONSULTANTS

WSP CANTOR SEINUK
STRUCTURAL
5301 BEETHOVEN STREET, SUITE 260
LOS ANGELES, CA 90066-7061
TEL: 310-578-0500
FAX: 310-578-1250

COSENTINI ASSOCIATES
MECHANICAL, ELECTRICAL, PLUMBING, FIRE PROTECTION & I.T
TWO PENNSYLVANIA PLAZA
NEW YORK, NY 10121
TEL: 212-615-3600
FAX: 212-615-3700

L'OBSERVATOIRE INTERNATIONAL
LIGHTING
474 WEST 14TH STREET, 5TH FLOOR
NEW YORK, NY 10014
TEL: 212-255-4463
FAX: 212-255-9346

McKAY CONANT BROOK INC.
ACOUSTICAL
5655 LINDERO CANYON ROAD, SUITE 325
WESTLAKE VILLAGE, CA 91362
TEL: 818-991-6300
FAX: 818-991-2324

EDGETT WILLIAMS CONSULTING GROUP, INC.
VERTICAL TRANSPORTATION
102 E. BLITHEDALE, SUITE 1
MILL VALLEY, CA 94941
TEL: 415-388-1890
FAX: 415-388-1860

SCHIRMER ENGINEERING
LIFE SAFETY
2231 S. WESTERN AVENUE, SUITE 100
TORRANCE, CA 90501
TEL: 310-782-0900
FAX: 310-782-1970

TRANSSOLAR
CLIMATE ENGINEER
145 HUDSON STREET
NEW YORK, NY 10013
TEL: 212-431-4318
FAX

DENEEN POWELL ATELIER, INC.
LANDSCAPE ARCHITECT
3300 EL CAJON BOULEVARD
SAN DIEGO, CA 92104
TEL: 619-294-9042
FAX: 619-294-9028

G.C. WALLACE, INC.
ENGINEERS, PLANNERS, SURVEYORS
1950 SOUTH RAINBOW BOULEVARD
LAS VEGAS, NEVADA 89146
TEL: 702-804-2000
FAX: 702-804-2299

LOU RUVO INSTITUTE
LAS VEGAS, NEVADA 89106

EXTERIOR
ELEVATIONS

PROJECT
2005-002
SCALE
1/8"=1'-0"
DRAWN BY
DATE
SEP. 23, 2005

SHEET NUMBER
A3-1.2

1 WEST ELEVATION
1/8"=1'-0"

2 EAST ELEVATION
1/8"=1'-0"

100% DESIGN DEVELOPMENT ISSUE
AUGUST 31, 2006

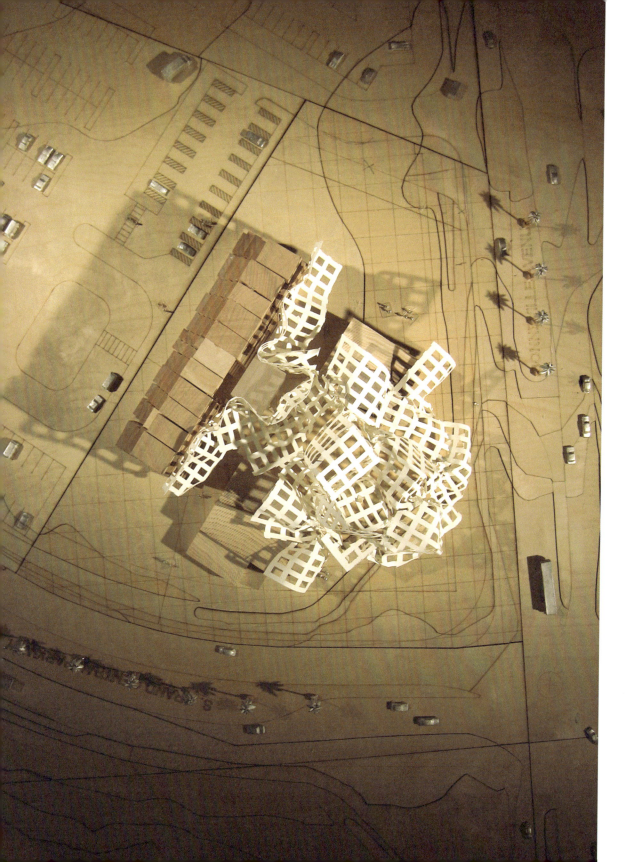

absent any ambiguity; but for the celebratory community hall, its deployment as a brash, high-spirited architectural matrix contradicts every one of those terms. Rationalism erupts into party-time; or, in Nietzschean nomenclature, the Apollonian goes Dionysian. The community hall, in Las Vegas-hospitality industry style, is intended to function in part as a rental space for a wide variety of private and public celebrations, with the income helping to fund the Ruvo Institute's research programs. So this witty and ingenious hybrid configuration gives unexpected, yet eloquent form to its unusual function.

Gehry often articulates different parts of his buildings with different materials; the changes not only break up the larger mass of the structure, they also help to identify interior functions hidden from the street. At Bilbao, for example, attention is usually focused on the glorious titanium skin, whose soft metallic panels seem to simultaneously absorb and reflect light, yielding a surface that virtually glows. (Has any other contemporary architect harnessed light more brilliantly than Gehry?) Metal clad-

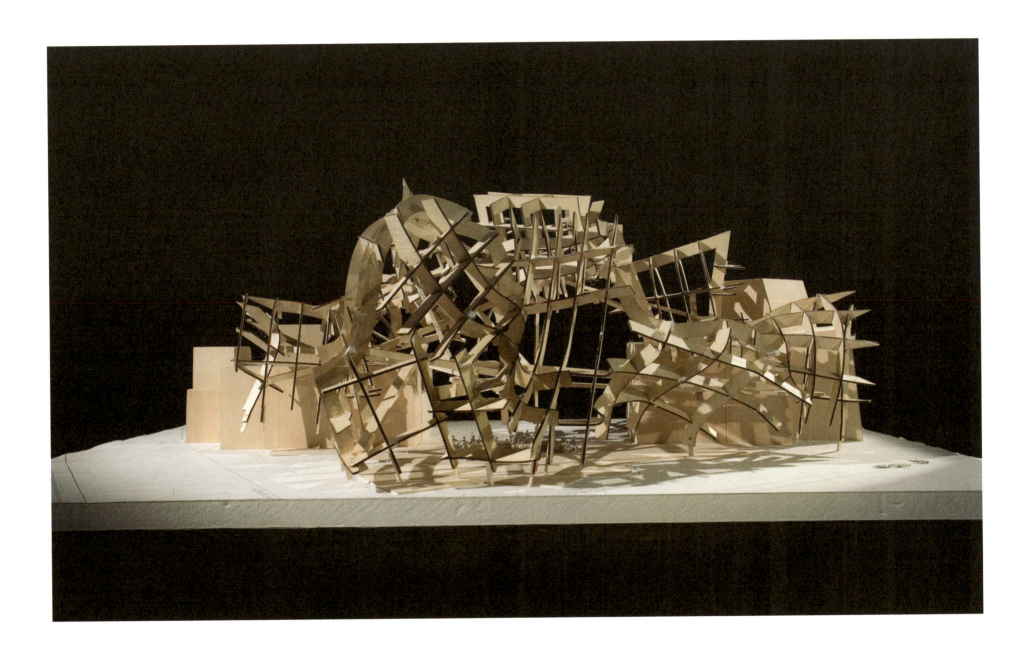

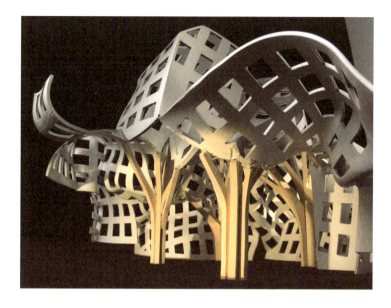

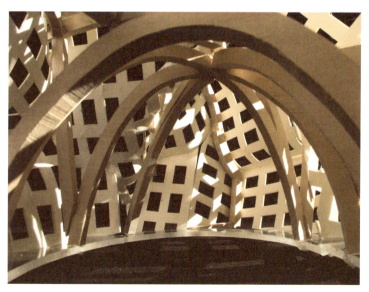

ding—from corrugated metal to lead-coated copper—has been a consistent element of Gehry's architecture since the late 1960s. But titanium was such an unprecedented choice that it garnered considerable attention when the Guggenheim Bilbao opened. What is not often noticed is that, in addition to the window glazing, the building is actually clad in three materials: not only thin panels of titanium, but limestone and painted stucco. Each material generally identifies a different building function: titanium for the museum's galleries, limestone for its public areas, and painted stucco for the administrative office block. Likewise, at the Disney Concert Hall in Los Angeles, buffed stainless steel is the cladding for the auditorium, highly polished stainless steel identifies the glittery patrons' room, and limestone articulates the building's podium and the rectangular block of administrative offices. (Disney Hall was designed earlier and influenced the Guggenheim Bilbao, although the latter was constructed first.)

In Las Vegas, the Apollonian-Dionysian dualism also extends to the building's two main functions. If the community hall on one side is exuberant, the examination rooms and offices on the other are more conventional—more orderly. I say "more" rather than "entirely" because nothing is ever black-and-white in Gehry World. Ambiguity is a source of the work's power, as it is for many great artists. The office wing is composed of a series of stacked rectilinear blocks whose arrangement follows the gentle curve of the street. The elevation is not flat, but syncopated—planes that advance and recede, according to the stacking of the blocks, instead of forming a smooth or continuous surface.

On the model, this elevation evokes something unexpected: the façade of the great, late-16th-century Roman church, Il Gesù, designed by Italian architect Giacomo della Porta. In the 1980s, a failed Postmodern style of architecture took the lamentable route of classical pastiche, featuring pilasters, volutes, twin pediments, niches, and other Greco-Roman motifs. Gehry's modern vocabulary of architectural forms for the Ruvo Institute is entirely different, eschewing phony classicism, but it is nonetheless baroque. Il Gesù marked a radical rupture

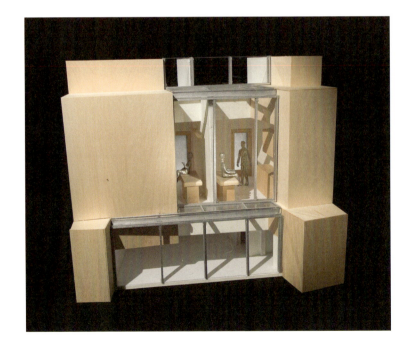

 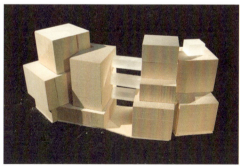 

with the High Renaissance—a milestone in the history of church architecture, and one of the most influential buildings before the modern era. In the philosophical battles of the Counter-Reformation, as the Church launched an aggressive campaign to propagate the faith, art and architecture were profoundly important ideological weapons. Builders became preoccupied with extreme physical size. Normal spatial limitations were disregarded. The microscope and the telescope were demonstrating that space is unified and unlimited, and Baroque architecture responded by reaching, stretching, and embracing amplitude. Freedom and spontaneity added a hitherto unexplored psychological dimension.

Della Porta's façade for Il Gesù is a pivot because of the way it set a static plane into visual motion. All the major horizontal elements of the entablature separating the first story from the second story are broken. As a result, the horizontals divide the big church

Giacomo della Porta Façade of Il Gesù, ca. 1575

into manageable parts, while unchecked verticals unify the two stories, making the building feel even larger and more imposing than it actually is. The five lateral bays across the front are not identical, in the manner of a classically ordered temple or High Renaissance palazzo. Instead, the bays become more three-dimensional as they approach the dramatic portal in the center. At the farthest edges the pilasters are flat. Moving inward they overlap, as if their flat planes are stepping forward; conversely, niches and doorways capped with pediments pierce the wall in the inner bays. Flanking the portal, which is crowned by an elaborate oval cartouche, rounded Corinthian columns replace the flat pilasters.

From the sides to the center, therefore, the façade makes a slight forward motion that reaches out toward the city. Il Gesù makes a gentle architectural gesture, inviting people to enter the grandly articulated door. That modest gesture would quickly become sensational in Baroque architecture. Size expanded dramatically—this is, after all, the era of gargantuan buildings like St. Peter's Cathedral, Blenheim Castle, the

Dresden Zwinger, and Versailles, the largest palace ever built—but its most effective examples always consider size in relation to the human subject. In its theatrical effort to impress, great Baroque architecture is always careful to consider and articulate human scale.

The dilemma of human scale precipitated one crisis in Modernist architecture that Gehry has been instrumental in resolving. The grid—a pure abstraction, as capable of continuous expansion as any modern industrial product, and without the possibility for the kinds of embellishment that classical architecture once provided—could (and often did) dehumanize built space. By contrast, the syncopated rectilinear façade of the Ruvo Institute's office wing, which breaks up the building's mass into a gentle arc of stacked bite-size chunks, is one inventive and charismatic formal solution to that nagging problem. Another is the undulating, folded stainless steel and glass grid of the community hall on the other side. The two sides embody different but related solutions to the same predicament. Each employs what might be called a Baroque

grid—a dynamic oxymoron to be sure, since it collapses the Apollonian and the Dionysian into a unified form, but one that seems appropriate to our topsy-turvy new millennium. Gehry's Baroque grid has the added virtue of embracing the instability, mutability, and disorder that is integral to nature and, not incidentally, to the drama of human experience.

Conceptually, it's not such a far distance from the paper-wrapped blocks of the eccentric study model to the more finished and conventional models for the $65-million building that will be erected as part of Las Vegas's mixed-use Union Park development. Practically, though, even with those elaborate models, the mind reels. How does one erect such seemingly impossible shapes in steel and glass, stone and stucco? How does one translate the model into plans and blueprints, which can be followed without undue puzzlement by the building trades? The answer, of course, is digital. First for the Barcelona fish, and most dramatically for the Bilbao museum, Gehry's office pioneered the use of a computer program originally designed for the French aerospace industry.

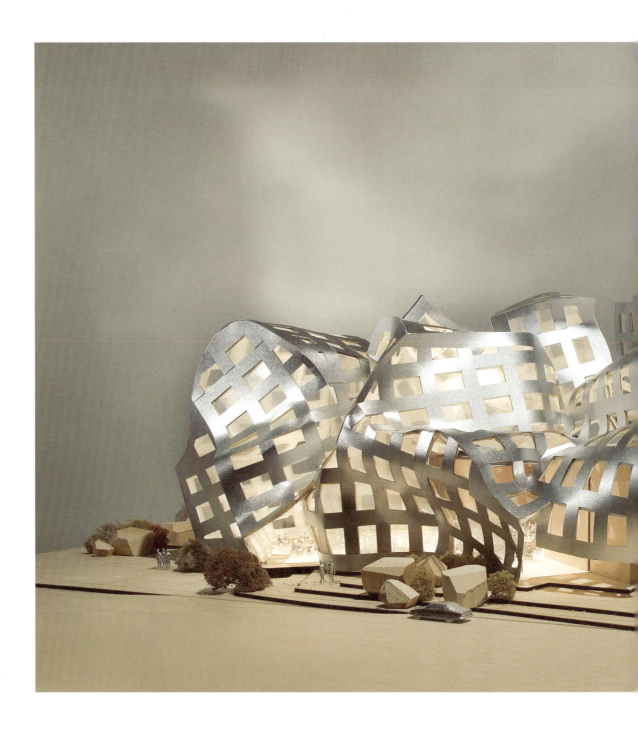

Since then, the program has been adapted and rewritten specifically to aid in Gehry's architectural design process. At his studio, there stands a gangly machine, which looks like something from a dentist's office. It is used to translate three-dimensional models into two-dimensional drawings. The tool, called a digitizer, employs a stylus at the end of a long arm. A technician traces the contours of the architectural model, and a computer reads the line that the stylus follows and draws it electronically.

During the haptic interface between stylus and model, the computer is sensing bodily movement, which it records in virtual space. In short, the mind is restored to the body. The computer is to Gehry's buildings what the telescope and microscope were to 16th- and 17th-century architecture, while digital code has replaced the lens. Apollo meets Dionysus in the electronic ether, with Gehry plotting their taut figures on the Ruvo Institute's stunning, multifarious Baroque grid.

There is profound poignancy in this—not least for a building associated with diseases that interrupt the neurological operations of the brain that control memory and motor functions. Remembrance might fuel Gehry's design process, but it is also an elusive phantom. The reason is plain: Like any great architect, he builds for the future, not the past. For both designer and patron, the Ruvo Institute makes manifest John Ruskin's claim about architecture's highest purpose and most sacred achievement: "See! This our fathers did for us."

In memory of Lolita Sarthou, whose grace was not diminished by her encounter with Alzheimer's disease.

Christopher Knight is chief art critic of the *Los Angeles Times*. He received the Frank Jewett Mather Award for Distinction in Art Criticism, was twice a finalist for the Pulitzer Prize in Criticism, and was a five-time recipient of the former Chemical Bank Award for Distinguished Newspaper Art Criticism. He is the author of *Last Chance for Eden: Selected Art Criticism, 1979-1994* and *Art of The Sixties and Seventies: The Panza Collection.*

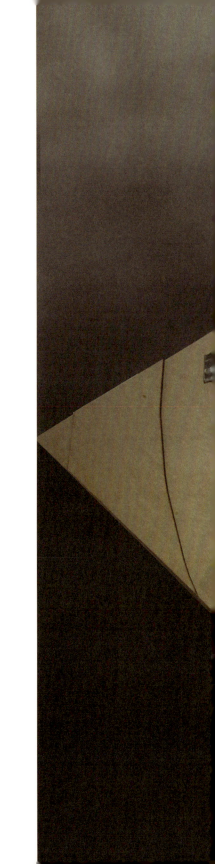

The Lou Ruvo Brain Institute

The design phase of Frank Gehry's Lou Ruvo Brain Institute is now complete. With groundbreaking imminent, and completion scheduled for 2008, the 65,000 square foot neuroscience research institute will become the first major "high architecture" building to rise in Las Vegas. Located on 1.9 acres at the entrance to the City of Las Vegas's 61-acre Union Park downtown redevelopment project, the Ruvo Institute will serve as the gateway to the mixed-use urban complex. The distinctive non-orthogonal, undulating lines of its "trellis" roof, which covers a large community hall and appears to cascade down from a gentle arc of rectilinear, stacked offices, will cut a striking profile against the soaring façades of The Related Companies' partially completed World Market Center Las Vegas, a home-furnishings trade showcase encompassing 12 million square feet in eight buildings. Other buildings in the park are still in the planning phase, including high-rise and townhouse residences, retail and service businesses, and a performing arts center.

From downtown, the Ruvo Institute will herald a radical change in architectural landscape that also will transform the look of the Las Vegas Strip, some five miles away. The Institute's distinctly sculptural, abstract design will stand in stark contrast to the scenographic casino resorts that presently line the Strip, even as the building becomes the first exterior expression of an aesthetic transition that originated inside major Strip resorts, in the 1990s. The first signs of change arrived with the haute-cuisine restaurateurs and designer clothiers who brought in their own internationally recognized decorators, and soon thereafter with the installation of sleek, 1970s-revival "ultra lounges," whose hip décor edged out the old-world styles that had predominated in Las Vegas nightclubs. In 2001, the transition gained momentum with the addition inside The Venetian Resort Hotel Casino of the Guggenheim Hermitage and Guggenheim Las Vegas museums, both designed by architect Rem Koolhaas. (Of particular note was the elaborate and dramatic inaugural exhibition installation in the Guggenheim Las Vegas, which

was designed by Frank Gehry himself.) The following year, THEhotel at Mandalay Bay opened with an urbane, Art Deco-inspired interior design enhanced with edgy contemporary art, setting a precedent in Las Vegas for fully integrating high design throughout the interior of an upscale hotel. Finally, in 2005, Las Vegas's most respected developer of resorts, Steve Wynn, opened his Wynn Las Vegas in a highly original and cultivated mix of traditional and innovative styles; this opening confirmed that Las Vegas had seen the last of the Disneyesque, theme-based resorts that, in the 1990s, had transformed the Strip into a compact, faux Grand Tour.

In the wake of the Ruvo Institute, Las Vegas will come closer to the promise of an Emerald City than ever before. MGM's new City Center, a huge hotel, residence, retail, and casino complex already under construction on the Strip, is scheduled for completion in 2009. It includes a 4,000-room Mandarin Oriental Hotel designed by Cesar Pelli, and the entire complex of shimmering glass buildings will be studded with fine contemporary art throughout. Just down the street, Fontainebleau Resorts's much anticipated Fontainebleau Las Vegas Hotel and Casino is planned as an innovative, seamless integration of fine contemporary art and high design that draws inspiration from Morris Lapidus's Miami resort architecture. And all over Las Vegas, stylish high-rise condominiums are opening their doors or are nearing completion. These and other coming attractions make clear that, from this point forward, the emphasis in Las Vegas aesthetics is on design-with-a-capital-D, and on architecture that competes at international levels of innovation and excellence.

The Ruvo Institute in Union Park also will emblematize the cultural change that is taking place as Las Vegas makes the transition from single-industry tourist playground to diversified urban metropolis. The new emphasis on high culture has strong support from City of Las Vegas Mayor Oscar Goodman, who has been directly overseeing the development of the Union Park project and a nearby downtown arts district. Clark County's Board of County Commissioners, recognizing the need to make cultural amenities available to Las Vegas's ever-expanding and increasingly gentrified population, also has stepped in to help philanthropic organizations fill the empty spaces where, in older communities of similar population and robust economy, research and arts entities already reside. The Ruvo Institute, which is dedicated to supporting the kind of research that could lead to cures for Alzheimer's, Parkinson's, Huntington's, ALS, and other diseases of the aging brain, will have the potential to make health-science contributions of global significance. The Ruvo Institute's building, designed by the world's most highly acclaimed architect, will make an immediate and decidedly significant contribution to the arts, providing Las Vegas with a landmark symbol of its cultural sophistication.

The establishment of the Ruvo Institute is due primarily to the organizing efforts of Larry Ruvo, who for many years has been interwoven in the social fabric of Las Vegas's business community. Known for his business acumen, sunny disposition, and generosity, Ruvo was raised in Las Vegas; he worked at Caesars Palace, and later at The Frontier, when these hotel-casinos opened their doors. He is the senior managing director of Nevada's largest wine, spirits, beer, and beverage distribution company, Southern Wine & Spirits of Nevada, a company with which Ruvo has been associated since 1969. Throughout his career, Ruvo has worked on behalf of a wide variety of charitable causes, spearheading the highly successful annual UNLVino wine-tasting event, which has raised millions of dollars to benefit students in The University of Nevada, Las Vegas's hotel administration programs. In 1999, he was honored with the Community Leadership Award by the national Points of Light Foundation, and has been recognized as Man of the Year by numerous Las Vegas charitable and business organizations.

In 1996, Ruvo established the Keep Memory Alive Foundation, with the goal of creating an institute dedicated to fostering collaborative efforts in the search for cures for neurodegenerative diseases. The foundation board includes an impressive roster of experts, among them Nancy Wexler. Dr. Wexler is president of the highly respected Hereditary Disease Foundation, with which Keep Memory Alive partners on workshop projects, and on whose board Frank Gehry has served for many years. It also includes the distinguished neuroscientist Leon Thal, who chairs the foundation's Medical and Scientific Advisory Board, and Zaven Khachaturian, the former director of the Office of Alzheimer's Research at the National Institutes of Health, who serves as Keep Memory Alive's president and CEO. Once constructed, the Ruvo Institute will no doubt stand as the flagship of Larry Ruvo's civic accomplishments; it is named in honor of Larry's father, Lou Ruvo, who for many years was a popular Las Vegas restaurateur, and who contracted Alzheimer's disease before he passed away in 1994.

The Las Vegas Art Museum strives to make its own contributions to Las Vegas's cultural landscape. Thus, it is a special privilege to present "Frank Gehry Designs the Lou Ruvo Brain Institute, Las Vegas." The exhibition features a comprehensive array of the models, sketches, renderings, plans, and other materials that represent all the developmental phases of design, from conceptualization, represented by an unexpected collection of inspirational photographs and crude models, to the detailed final model and renderings. To complete the picture, I traveled to Los Angeles for an interview with Frank Gehry, Larry Ruvo, and Zaven Khachaturian. I met up with the three on August 24, 2006, as they were leaving a 98th birthday party for Milton Wexler, founder of the Hereditary Disease Foundation. Our conversation took place at The Hump restaurant in Santa Monica. Over dinner, it quickly became apparent that the three men, of widely diverse backgrounds, are closely united in their passion to advance scientific discovery in fields related to neurodegenerative diseases, and that Frank Gehry brings more to the cause than a stellar design for a groundbreaking building.

—Libby Lumpkin, Director

Interview with Frank Gehry, Zaven Khachaturian, and Larry Ruvo

Santa Monica, California
August 24, 2006

Libby Lumpkin

Let's start at the beginning. Larry, you're creating an institute dedicated to finding cures for Alzheimer's and other diseases of the mind. You've secured a site in downtown Las Vegas. You need a building. How did you decide to ask Frank Gehry to design it? Did you make a short list?

Larry Ruvo

I had a short list, but the only person that I had a serious interest in—the only one I conceptualized—was Frank. He was my number one choice, and the only architect I ever talked to about it.

Libby Lumpkin

Did you know Frank, or did you just make a cold call?

Larry Ruvo

Basically, it was a cold call. I wrote a letter to a fellow I know who once worked for Frank. Frank's office told me I could have 45 minutes with him. Two-and-a-half hours into the meeting, we were still together. And there was this bond, this instant…

Frank Gehry

Yeah, it was amazing. Pure chemistry.

Larry Ruvo

At the end of the meeting, Frank said: "Come back in two weeks, and I'll tell you if I'm going to do this building." I walked out of his studio and felt that I had found a new brother, a pal, a colleague, and a confidant. At that point,

there was never any question about who might be number two. I wanted Frank Gehry, and no one else. When I came back two weeks later, I totally let my guard down. Frank walks right in and says: "I'm going to do the building." And that was it.

Frank Gehry

My only hesitation was scheduling. I wanted to design the building from the day I met Larry, but I had to figure it out. I had partners then, and I had to consider other factors.

Libby Lumpkin

So, Frank, no hesitations about building in Las Vegas, a city with its own distinctive entertainment architecture? You had turned down projects in Las Vegas before, hadn't you?

Frank Gehry

No hesitations. I feel totally comfortable building in Las Vegas. My father was in the slot-machine business in Canada when I was a kid. I grew up with gambling. I'm not a gambler myself, but I'm comfortable with people in the business. It's true that I had turned down projects in Las Vegas before, but that was because the people who wanted to hire me already knew what they wanted in terms of design. They know their stuff, and have been successful with their own designs. They wanted control. I wanted control. Although I like the people involved very much, it never worked out.

The creative process is not something you can plan. It's sort of opportunistic. Something happens, you take advantage of it, and it unfolds. When Larry came to me, I thought: "My god. This tiny little building for medical research, on a topic close to my heart. What a wonderful way to show Las Vegas that I don't hate the city." Before Larry, I didn't see how I could contribute to Las Vegas. But in this case, I felt I could, so I was willing.

Larry Ruvo

I never heard Frank explain why he rejected Las Vegas projects before. It's very interesting. I have learned that when I work with people who know their fields, I should be quiet and listen. I think Frank understood that I trusted him to design the building. In my own profession—food and beverage—I've tried to be on top of everything, because I know the distribution business. I know what I can sell, and I know what works. Architecture is not my business. I take no credit for Frank's design. Zero. Just like the roulette wheel has two zeros, I am double zeros on this design.

Zaven Khachaturian

The analogy is Renaissance Florence. Larry is Lorenzo the Magnificent, and Frank is Michelangelo. Lorenzo basically gave carte blanche to Michelangelo, as well as to scholars and writers of the time, and Larry has given carte blanche to Frank to design the building. And he has given me carte blanche to organize a new approach to not only cure diseases of the brain, but to solve the mysteries of the mind. Neuroscience is the next great frontier. It's more exciting to me than space exploration or subatomic physics. Understanding the mind is our greatest challenge. Larry and Frank are setting the stage for a total transformation, another Renaissance. And it's happening in Las Vegas.

Libby Lumpkin

Frank, you say the Ruvo Institute project is close to your heart…

Frank Gehry

My connection is through Milton Wexler, a psychologist.

Libby Lumpkin

Whose 98th birthday party you all attended this afternoon?

Frank Gehry

Yes. I've been a trustee of Milton's Hereditary Disease Foundation for some 35 years. Actually, the artist Ed Moses brought him to me many years ago, when Ed saw me struggling with life at a certain point. Ed was worried about me. Within two years, Milton turned my life around. We just talked. He set me straight on so many things, even got me to quit smoking. Milton always has had a special interest in artists; he has devoted one-third of his practice to treating artists for free. That's why I first went to him. At the time, I couldn't afford help otherwise. We quickly became close friends.

Three or four years after I met Milton, his wife was diagnosed with Huntington's disease. His daughters were in their 30s, and it was fifty-fifty that they would contract the disease as well. Milton decided to do something about it. He had a relationship with the scientist Linus Pauling, who was doing studies for schizophrenia with vinegar and amino acids. Milton got Pauling, Seymour Benzer—the biologist who did the famous gene experiments with fruit flies at CalTech—and another fellow working on Parkinson's, and several scientists from the National Institutes of Health. With them, Milton and his daughter, Nancy Wexler, sort of invented the workshop approach to mental disease. It's been a very effective tool. That's what we bring to the pot, right Larry?

Larry Ruvo

Frank, you bring many important ingredients. Nancy and Milton Wexler have been very important to the organization. Nancy is also the president of the Hereditary Disease Foundation, now that Milton is less active, and she teaches neuropsychology at Columbia University. She did a study with a Venezuelan family that led to the discovery of the gene for Huntington's. That discovery was a major breakthrough.

Zaven Khachaturian

Besides that, the Hereditary Disease Foundation brings a lot of scientific intellectual prowess.

Frank Gehry

Back when Milton was putting together his foundation, he asked me to design a building for it. I got all excited. I was going to do a building for science! That sort of thing is really important for a young architect. Then the board—all these scientists—had their first meeting and decided they should do an institute without walls! [Laughter.] So, I was eliminated. I stayed with the group, however, became a trustee and helped them over the years. I'm still very active in it. Milton was always involving me in symposia that brought together artists and scientists. We never understood each other; whatever we learned, it wasn't because we could speak each other's language. Yet, we could sense that we were all working creatively.

Zaven Khachaturian

That's what the Ruvo Institute will do, bring scientists working in many different areas together. The silos that separate scientists today are no longer viable. The Ruvo Institute will, for the first time, bring the study of all neurodegenerative diseases together. We will do something that hasn't been done before: create a worldwide network of collaborations. We will bring together all the different disciplines—genetics, biology, epidemiology, ethics—to explore the human mind through a systems approach. This model of solving problems, the systems approach, found great success with the Manhattan Project, which brought together people from fields as diverse as engineering, physics, and carpentry. This also is the philosophy of the Ruvo Institute. Imagine you have all of the best players in the NFL in one game…

Libby Lumpkin

An "All Star Team"?

Zaven Khachaturian

Right. That's what we bring to Las Vegas.

Larry Ruvo

A critical part of my relationship with Zaven and my friend Leon Thal—a neuroscientist at U.C. San Diego, who's also on the board of Keep Memory Alive—is total trust. I don't request daily reports. I listen, admire, and try to understand. But they don't have to explain to me what they are doing in detail. You don't hire experts to tell experts what to do. You hire the best and let them be the best.

Zaven Khachaturian

This really is a formula for success, whether it's used in building a structure, painting a canvas, or doing scientific research. A patron has a vision, makes a commitment, finds the right people, and then gets out of the way. The Manhattan Project proceeded in this manner, as did Kennedy's space program.

Larry Ruvo

Another more recent example is Severe Acute Respiratory Syndrome, or SARS. The cure for SARS was found in three or four months.

Zaven Khachaturian

Yes. That's the model we are using.

Libby Lumpkin

Larry, the Lou Ruvo Brain Institute is named for your late father, who suffered from Alzheimer's. After he died, you created the Keep Memory Alive Foundation to raise funds for Alzheimer's research. Did you create the foundation with the Ruvo Institute in mind?

Larry Ruvo

My dad died of Alzheimer's in 1994, on February 18th. He was my best friend in life. I just loved this man. He was a real street guy, and very knowledgeable. He taught me everything I know about business. It's a great story how Keep Memory Alive came to be. After Dad died—three or four months later—some of our friends said: "Your father loved food and wine. He should have a going-away party—a dinner party." So, about 35 or 40 of us got together upstairs at Wolfgang Puck's restaurant in Caesars Palace. A buddy of mine comes in, not knowing we were there. They send him up to us, and he asks me what we're doing. I said: "We're having a dinner for Lou." He said: "I want to give $5,000 to Alzheimer's." It wasn't a fundraiser! But that $5,000 turned into a lot of money that night. We didn't know what to do with it at first. So, we called an Alzheimer's center, and the rest, as they say…

Libby Lumpkin
So, Keep Memory Alive came to be by an accident of fate.

Larry Ruvo
One of its unsung heroes is Wolfgang Puck, who is one of the most generous people I've ever met. After that dinner for my dad, Wolfgang offered to do another, larger affair. He closed his restaurant for an evening and brought in Nobu Matsuhisa. We raised a great deal of money that night, and Wolfgang's been with us every year since. Now there will be a Wolfgang Puck restaurant in a Frank Gehry building, with everything in the restaurant designed by Frank—chairs, tables, everything. We'll be able to rent the community hall for a facilities fee, and that money will help fund the Institute and our research programs.

Libby Lumpkin
So, having a building designed by Frank Gehry helps the Ruvo Institute achieve its mission?

Larry Ruvo
The Frank Gehry building is raising the money to create the Institute. We'll be successful because of Frank. The building has raised way more money than Zaven ever dreamed. If it were a regular building, it probably wouldn't get built at all.

Zaven Khachaturian
That's right. Frank is creating an icon, in the way that I.M. Pei's building is an icon for the Buck Institute in Marin County, and Louis Kahn's building is an icon for the Salk Institute in La Jolla. The building will have symbolic meaning, in the way that Renaissance buildings convey meanings. Frank's building generates value beyond its physical presence.

Libby Lumpkin
Frank, I've seen the two-part design of your building described as a metaphor for brain disease, the rectilinear, stacked offices on one side representing the healthy mind, and the undulating trellis that seems to be sort of collapsing down on top of the other side as the intrusion of brain disease. Would you agree with this description?

Frank Gehry
I'm not bothered by the description, but it's not at all what I intended. Maybe I unconsciously designed it that way—like a scrambled mind—but the way I arrived at the design was very different. I was designing a trellis to cover a large garden room, to be used for conferences and parties. I started out by making sketches of gardens and trellises.

Libby Lumpkin
Larry, what was your reaction when you first saw the collapsing trellis design? It's very distinctive.

Larry Ruvo
When I first saw the model, my heart stopped. I will admit that.

Frank Gehry
Just think about this: I bring in a model that looks like an explosion. Larry looks at the model. He looks at me. He didn't miss a beat.

Larry Ruvo
True.

Frank Gehry

Larry said: "Boy that's…" Well, I forget exactly what he said, but he didn't say anything negative. I knew what he was thinking—and even said so, I think.

Larry Ruvo

Yes, you did.

Frank Gehry

I said: "Just hang in there. We'll get there. It'll be okay. People are going to say funny things about it. When the Disney Hall model was first shown, the letters to the editor called it 'broken crockery.' I'm used to that." [Laughter.] Every time I do something, somebody says something peculiar about it.

Libby Lumpkin

The trellis hall consumes roughly half of the building. Did the three of you conceptualize the room together?

Frank Gehry

Larry told me what he wanted. Both Larry and Mayor Oscar Goodman said that they wanted me to make something that stands out in Las Vegas. I heard that several times: "It's got to stand out." So, I said to them: "How do you design a building in Las Vegas that stands out? You know, everything's been done, everything's been corrupted. It's like Times Square with all the lights. How the hell do you make something stand out unless you create an explosion of some kind?!" [Laughter.] So, I started messing with the trellis, re-forming it with my hands. I loved the tactile feeling of it. I made some blocks in wood, then I took paper with window cuts in it that I had been using on other buildings—I really love that paper—and bunched it over the model. And it took off! I made several models that way, but it could never be built. If I designed it that way in the end, I would have blown the budget.

Libby Lumpkin

Christopher Knight opens his essay for the catalog, which you haven't yet seen, with a description of that first, crumpled-paper model. He describes it as "a little lump of 'creative play.'" Is your method of designing a form of creative play?

Frank Gehry

Every artist I know engages in some form of creative play. Robert Rauschenberg does. Jasper Johns does. But I wasn't using crumpled paper for crumpled paper's sake. I was forming it over blocks that represented exactly the program of the building. It was willful. The design flowed from that.

Libby Lumpkin

But your initial design was too expensive to build?

Frank Gehry

Right. The first version was so crumpled you couldn't build it. It looked beautiful, but it had deep crevasses in it, and other impractical shapes. So, I started to rationalize it, but when I did, I lost its essence somewhat. I asked Craig Webb in my studio to take a shot at straightening it out. I was so enamored with its basic design, it probably would have been hard for me to change it on my own. After Craig did the rationalization, I took it to the final step.

Libby Lumpkin

When I was in your studio, I noticed you had "concept" photographs tacked up in areas where you were in the beginning stages of a project. I asked your assistant if you had used photographs to help conceptualize the Ruvo Institute, and was shown an assortment of images of nature scenes, and some of early tribal buildings, most of them shot from above.

Frank Gehry

I probably picked up a book during this period—again, it's opportunism—and the photographs related to what we were doing with the building. They were just to look at. Images like those are always inspirational.

Libby Lumpkin

You have over 150 assistants in your studio. Are you happy with such a large operation—with presiding over an empire?

Frank Gehry

Yes, but I don't treat the studio like an empire. I play with the guys. As Christopher Knight says, my work is fundamentally a kind of creative play. It's fun to be a hummingbird. I go from one project to another. If I only had one or two jobs, I would go nuts, because my attention would be focused on them too intensely; I would overwork them. With lots of projects in development at the same time, I get pulled. I have people waiting for me to make a decision. And, making decisions is good, because it's like a commitment. You have to learn to make commitments. It's like being confident that when you get up from a chair you can step there, and then take another step, and another…you make a commitment to move ahead. You start making decisions, and the project evolves from that.

Libby Lumpkin

May I ask about the columns inside the trellis hall, which are shaped like trees? What was your decision-making process regarding those?

Frank Gehry

The tree-like form is the simplest column to spread the load.

Libby Lumpkin

I was hoping for a more colorful explanation.

Frank Gehry

I know. But it's standard engineering.

Libby Lumpkin

In the models, the trellis appears to be quite thick, but it seems lightweight. What will it be made of?

Frank Gehry

It's structural steel, and some of it is a foot deep, or maybe eighteen inches. In order to plug the glass in it, you have to waterproof it and put a casing over it. That's what makes it look so thick. The idea of something heavy that in fact looks very light interests me greatly.

Libby Lumpkin

Sort of like the 17th-century Italian Baroque sculptor Bernini, who could make marble look like gossamer silk. Come to think of it, the undulating shape of the trellis is a bit like Bernini drapery. Do you look at Bernini?

Frank Gehry

I look at Bernini a lot.

Libby Lumpkin

That's always a pleasure.

Frank Gehry

I'll tell you a Bernini story. I go to Rome at least once a year, right? So, every time I go, I visit Bernini's *Ecstacy of St. Teresa*. Now, *St. Teresa* is in a small church, the Santa Maria della Vittoria. There are these pews that come to here [Frank points to an imaginary floorplan on the table], and the altar is here, in front of the pews. That's where *St. Teresa* is. But you can't go there during Mass; you have to stay back, on the other side of the pews. So, in order to see *St. Teresa*, you have to go like this [Frank leans forward and cranes his neck]. And even that does not give you a good view. Every time I've gone to the church, there's a Mass, and some guy won't let me pass! So, I go sit in the pews, and do the Mass. I do this year after year. Eventually, one of the priests became suspicious of me, and he gives me a look. I'm sure he recognized me. But I don't cop to it. I do the sign of the cross, I kneel, I sing. I do it all, but I do everything wrong. The last time I was there, that priest was just giggling. By now, he knows me, and he is very sweet about it all. So, do I look at Bernini? Yes.

Libby Lumpkin

The renderings of the interior of the trellis hall show dramatic light effects. Were you thinking of how the light would fall in the interior when you designed the trellis?

Frank Gehry

Yes, yes. That's the whole game. The renderings show the light effects as the sun goes around, with the sunlight streaming in. It'll be a really beautiful space. During the day, we might have to do some shading, a kind of photovoltaic system to manage the light.

Libby Lumpkin

How do you want the visitor to feel in the hall? Are you after the beautiful or the sublime—pleasure or emotion?

Frank Gehry

Comfort and pleasure—and infinite interest. It should never look the same, like the sea. The room will be constantly changing, but in a natural way that will make it a memorable experience—not just an experience, but a *memorable* experience. People are not going to forget being in that room. I want it to be incredibly exciting and beautiful—and new, like nothing they've experienced before, such that people can't take their eyes off it, and they want to come back, and will want to remember the room. That's what Larry asked me to do, to make a place in Las Vegas that will be memorable.

Gianlorenzo Bernini *The Ecstasy of Saint Teresa*, 1645-52

Libby Lumpkin

Keep memory alive?

Frank Gehry

That's what it is, exactly. The logo is Keep Memory Alive, and I'm trying to make a building that people will want to visit, remember, talk about, and enjoy—and ultimately will want to partner with us at the Institute to help cure some of the neurodegenerative diseases. Now, that's a lot to ask of a building, a small building by Las Vegas standards. But I like to deliver what I'm asked to do. That's why we call it the "mouse that roared."

Larry Ruvo

That's right.

Frank Gehry

There's a lot of love going into this building. You can't quantify it. You could never predict that Larry and I would get along—you know, like and respect each other the way we do.

Zaven Khachaturian

That's a story in itself.

Frank Gehry

I instantly trusted Larry.

Larry Ruvo

And I instantly trusted Frank. I never said this to Frank, but I'll say it now. I gave Frank Gehry the single most important thing in my life, the reputation of my father's name. There's nothing more important to me. Think about it, our whole circle of life is about friendship and trust. I had no better friend than my father. I said: "Here Frank, here's my father's name. Make me proud." And he went beyond that trust. What Frank Gehry has done for me, I will never forget.

Illustrations

For irregularly shaped objects, all dimensions are listed.

Unless otherwise indicated, all illustrations depict sketches, models, renderings, or plans produced in 2005 and 2006 and are courtesy of Gehry Partners, LLP.

Design Partner: Frank Gehry
Project Partner: Terry Bell
Project Architects: David Rodriguez, Michal Sedlacek
Project Designer: Brian Zamora
Project Team: Eun Sung Chang, Natalie Magarian, Yvon Romeus, Ronald Rosell, Sarah David, Andrew Galambos, Natalie Milberg, Sameer Kashyap, Kurt Komraus, Marc Bonds, Kumiko Koda, Frederic Herbere, Scott Carter

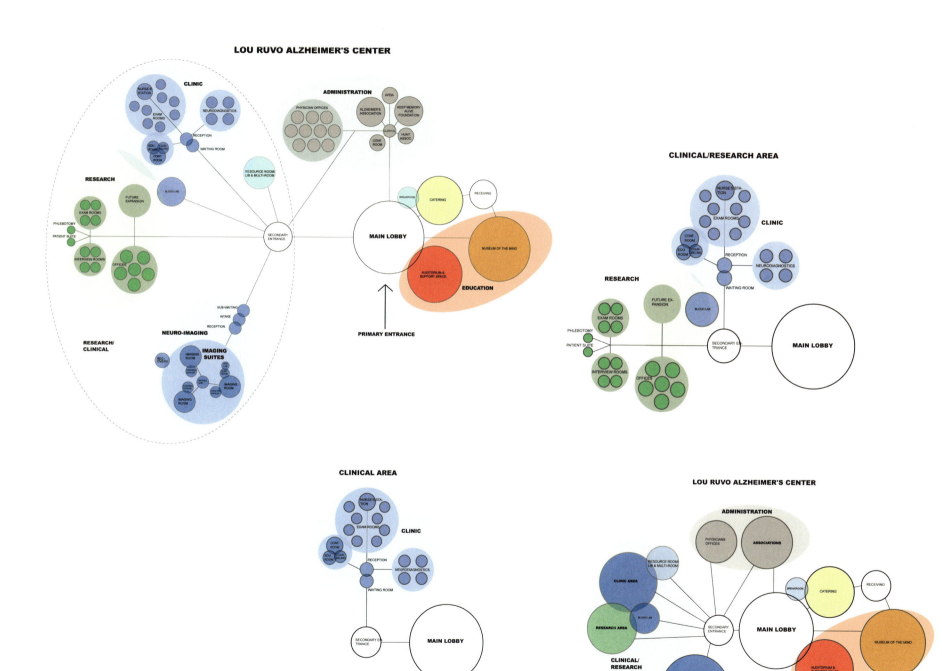

LOU RUVO ALZHEIMER'S CENTER

CLINIC

NURSE'S STATION

EXAM ROOMS

NEURODIAGNOSTICS

EDU ROOM

COUNSELING

CONF ROOM

RECEPTION

WAITING ROOM

ADMINISTRATION

PHYSICIAN OFFICES

ALZHEIMER'S ASSOCIATION

APDA

KEEP MEMORY ALIVE FOUNDATION

CLERICAL

CONF ROOM

HUNT ASSOC

RESOURCE ROOM/ LIB & MULTI-ROOM

RESEARCH

EXAM ROOMS

FUTURE EXPANSION

BLOOD LAB

PHLEBOTOMY

PATIENT SUITE

INTERVIEW ROOMS

OFFICES

SECONDARY ENTRANCE

BREAKROOM

CATERING

RECEIVING

MAIN LOBBY

MUSEUM OF THE MIND

AUDITORIUM & SUPPORT SPACE

EDUCATION

PRIMARY ENTRANCE

SUB-WAITING

INTAKE

RECEPTION

NEURO-IMAGING

RESEARCH/ CLINICAL

RECOVERY

IMAGING ROOM

CONTROL ROOM

STAFFING LOUNGE

CONTROL ROOM

READ

PROCESS OFFICE

CONTROL ROOM

IMAGING SUITES

IMAGING ROOM

IMAGING ROOM

CLINICAL/RESEARCH AREA

NURSE'S STATION

EXAM ROOMS

CLINIC

CONF ROOM

EDU ROOM

COUNSELING

RECEPTION

NEURODIAGNOSTICS

WAITING ROOM

RESEARCH

EXAM ROOMS

FUTURE EXPANSION

BLOOD LAB

PHLEBOTOMY

PATIENT SUITE

INTERVIEW ROOMS

OFFICES

SECONDARY ENTRANCE

MAIN LOBBY

CLINICAL AREA

NURSE'S STATION

EXAM ROOMS

CLINIC

CONF ROOM

EDU ROOM

COUNSELING

RECEPTION

NEURODIAGNOSTICS

WAITING ROOM

SECONDARY ENTRANCE

MAIN LOBBY

LOU RUVO ALZHEIMER'S CENTER

ADMINISTRATION

PHYSICIANS OFFICES

ASSOCIATIONS

RESOURCE ROOM LIB & MULTI-ROOM

CLINIC AREA

BREAKROOM

CATERING

RECEIVING

RESEARCH AREA

BLOOD LAB

SECONDARY ENTRANCE

MAIN LOBBY

CLINICAL/ RESEARCH

NEUROIMAGING AREA

AUDITORIUM & SUPPORT SPACE

MUSEUM OF THE MIND

EDUCATION

PRIMARY ENTRANCE

Acknowledgements

Only a few years ago, the arrival of a Frank Gehry building in Las Vegas seemed but a distant dream. Today, it is a tangible reality. With groundbreaking only weeks away, the Lou Ruvo Brain Institute soon will become Las Vegas's most distinguished edifice. The Las Vegas Art Museum is pleased to celebrate this milestone with "Frank Gehry Designs the Lou Ruvo Brain Institute, Las Vegas." The exhibition offers a preview of the building's distinctive design and an opportunity to examine in depth the path of the creative imagination that led to it.

The organization of this exhibition began the hard way, with the prospect of well over 100 design objects, most so recently created that they had not been photographed, archived, or ordered. In the process of pulling the exhibition together, I have run up the tally of people to thank. At the top of the list is Frank Gehry.

A split-second glance at the buzzing activity and ambitious projects underway inside the Gehry Partners studio in Marina Del Rey, California, tells you that Mr. Gehry is a very busy man. Thus, I owe him a special debt for so graciously sharing his time and making his staff available. Ruvo Institute project designer Brian Zamora has been indispensable in reconstructing a chronology of the project and making sense of often unfamiliar material, and studio archivist Laura Stella has spent many hours preparing objects for reproduction in the catalog and for transport to LVAM.

Tom and Bonnie Lawyer arranged for the generous support provided by their company Lawyer Trane, which has made LVAM's presentation of the Frank Gehry exhibition possible. As a member of the LVAM Board of Trustees, and President of the LVAM Foundation Board of Trustees, Tom Lawyer provides continuing and hands-on support for Museum operations.

Larry Ruvo's reputation for generosity is fully deserved. Mr. Ruvo brought us the idea of the exhibition and arranged for much of the support that has made it possible. When I requested an interview with him, together with Frank Gehry and Zaven Khachaturian, he found the slot of time that all could gather, and arranged for transportation. As the driving force behind the creation of the Ruvo Institute, the entire city of Las Vegas owes him a debt of gratitude.

LVAM is most delighted to have provided in this catalog an opportunity for art critic Christopher Knight's insightful ideas to sparkle brilliantly; he has concisely and eloquently grasped the essence of Frank Gehry's "creative play." Mr. Knight's essay is complemented by the catalog itself, which is edited by Gary Kornblau. Mr. Kornblau conceptualized the catalog under impossible deadlines and directed the superb design created by Skeet Link. Thanks also to Eric Olsen of Bright City Books and Martin Fox for editing support.

LVAM staff has rallied to face unique challenges. Deputy Director Renee Coppola and Registrar Courtney Howerton contributed substantial and expert curatorial services on the project; Education Assistant Katie Anania developed the educational materials that serve the teachers and schoolchildren of Southern Nevada. Development Director Stephanie Salamah and team members Michele Jones and Charlotte Matthews have brought professional grace to generating support for the exhibition and planning special accompanying events.

A special note of thanks to James Zeiter, who has supported this project in every way. As president of LVAM's Board of Trustees, Mr. Zeiter steers the ship. He keeps us motoring on, while steadily, politely, and diligently pointing us in the right direction.

Finally, I would like to thank the LVAM Members whose names appear on the following list. These enlightened patrons represent the community strength of our organization. They make it possible for LVAM to present exhibitions that promote the Museum's efforts to join the international community of significant museums of contemporary art and design.

—Libby Lumpkin, Director

Frank Gehry Designs
The Lou Ruvo Brain Institute, Las Vegas

Las Vegas Art Museum
December 13, 2006 – March 25, 2007

is presented by

with sponsorship provided by

Partner Sponsors
Joyce Mack
Southern Wine & Spirits of America

Patron Sponsors
American Nevada Company
Bruce & Nancy Deifik
Eureka Casinos
Insight Holdings, LLC
Keep Memory Alive
Doris & Ted Lee, Dana & Greg Lee
Manpower, Inc. of Southern Nevada
Southern Wine & Spirits of Nevada
StorageOne

Las Vegas Art Museum Patrons

LVAM Benefactor

American Nevada Company
Hannah An
Bruce & Nancy Deifik
Donald W. Reynolds Foundation
Patrick Duffy & Wally Goodman
Eureka Casinos
Robin & Daniel Greenspun

James & Joan Hammer
Harko Family Trust
Andy Katz
Lawyer Trane
Roger Thomas & Arthur Libera
Doris & Ted Lee, Dana & Greg Lee
Joyce Mack

Mark & Hilarie Moore
Martin Mull
James & Heather Murren
Pierre & Pamela Omidyar
Donald Rosenfeld
Glenn & Renee Schaeffer
Jordan Schnitzer

Dick & Vicki Hafen Scott
Southern Wine & Spirits of America
Southern Wine & Spirits of Nevada
StorageOne
James & Michelle Zeiter

President's Circle

Timothy & Lisa McCarthy,
    Southern Wine & Spirits

Blanche & Philip Meisel
MGM Mirage

Nevada Arts Council

John & Irene Smith,
    DeLuca Liquor & Wine

Director's Circle

Karen Barrett & Gerald Facciani
John Blackmon, SouthwestUSA Bank
Heather & Todd duBoef
Barbara Greenspun
Myra & Brian Greenspun
Chris & Katie Holmen

Tom & Bonnie Lawyer
The Molasky Group of Companies
David & Laura Taylor Mulkey
Michael Niarchos
Nevada Trust Company
Jerry & Lotty Polis

James & Beverly Rogers
Steven Rosenberg
Frank Schreck
Harry Shull
Tim & Jane Snow
John U. Tippins IV

Barry & Kathryn Thalden
Parry & Peggy Thomas
Tom Thomas
Aurora & Buck Wong

Curator's Circle

Janice & Fred Allen
Curt & Susan Anderson
Naomi Arin
Florence Bolatin
Zoe Brown
Bulbman, Inc.
Arthur Curtis
Patricia & A.C. D'Augustine
Judith & Patrick DeMoon

Audrey Dempsey
Bill & Miriam English
Teresa Eyre
Susan Fine
Jeff & Jane Gale
Russell & Karen Goldsmith
Guggenheim Hermitage Museum
Tony Illia
Penn & Emily Jillette

Timothy & Karen Kimball
James & Barbara Lamdin
Elaine Lewis
Meg MacFarlane
Virginia & Mark V. Martino
Frank Martin
Barbara Molasky
James Stanford & Julia Morris
Daniel & Araceli Mulcahy

Betty Pardo, Ph.D.
Diana & Kenneth Record
Tom Schoeman & Bridget Whitehurst
Tom Smiley
William & Ann Sullivan
Bunny & Jay Wasserman
Eugene & Lai Wong
Irene & David Wu

These images are among a number of photographs used for inspiration during the conceptual phase in the design development of the Lou Ruvo Brain Institute.

Colophon

This catalog was printed at Typecraft Wood & Jones Lithography in Cochin Regular with heads in Helvetica Neue UltraLight on Finch Fine Brilliant White, an acid-free paper certified by the Forest Stewardship Council and guaranteed to come from forests managed to conserve biodiversity.

Catalog design by Skeet Link.

Left: **Laurence Mouton** *Morocco, Palm Grove and Mountainside Village* © Laurence Mouton/PhotoAlto/Getty Images
Right: **Tom Bean** *Cross-Bedded Sandstone Formations* © Tom Bean/CORBIS